Upside

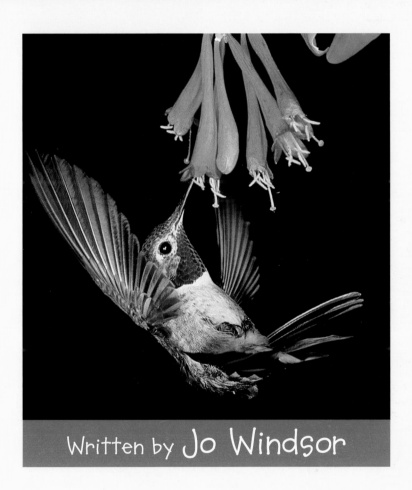

Written by Jo Windsor

The fly can go
upside down.

The bat can go
upside down.

The bee can go
upside down.

The spider can go
upside down.

The caterpillar can go
upside down.

The bird can go
upside down.

14

Index

Guide Notes

Title: Upside Down

Stage: Emergent – Magenta

Genre: Nonfiction (Expository)

Approach: Guided Reading

Processes: Thinking Critically, Exploring Language, Processing Information

Written and Visual Focus: Photographs (static images), Illustrations, Index

Word Count: 36

READING THE TEXT

Tell the children that this book is about some animals that can appear to go "upside down." Talk to them about what is on the front cover. Read the title and the author.

Focus the children's attention on the index and talk about the animals that are in this book. "Walk" through the book, focusing on the photographs and talk about the different animals that are upside down.

Read the text together.

THINKING CRITICALLY
(sample questions)
- What other animals can go upside down?
- Why would animals go upside down?

EXPLORING LANGUAGE
(ideas for selection)

Terminology
Title, cover, author, photographs, illustrations

Vocabulary
Interest words: bee, bat, fly, spider, caterpillar, bird
High-frequency words: the, can, go